Changing Weather

Sharon Coan

Publishing Credits

Rachelle Cracchiolo, M.S.Ed., *Publisher*
Conni Medina, M.A.Ed., *Managing Editor*
Jamey Acosta, *Content Director*
Dona Herweck Rice, *Series Developer*
Robin Erickson, *Multimedia Designer*

Image Credits: Cover, p.1 ©iStock.com/Borut Trdina; p.3 ©iStock.com/Grabpa; pp.4, 12 ©iStock.com/Beth Shepherd Peters; p.5, Back cover ©iStock.com/urbancow; pp.6, 12 ©iStock.com/AVTG; p.7 ©iStock.com/carterdayne; pp.9, 12 ©iStock.com/Erkki Makkonen; p.10 ©iStock.com/DenisTangneyJr; p.11 iStock.com/kelly civitarese; all other images from Shutterstock.

Library of Congress Cataloging-in-Publication Data

Coan, Sharon, author.
  Changing weather / Sharon Coan.
    pages cm
  Summary: "The weather is always changing. In this book you will see some of those changes"--Provided by publisher.
  Audience: K to grade 3.
  ISBN 978-1-4938-2054-2 (pbk.)
  1. Weather--Juvenile literature. I. Title.
  QC981.3.C626 2016
  551.6--dc23
                                                              2015011887

Teacher Created Materials

5301 Oceanus Drive
Huntington Beach, CA 92649-1030
http://www.tcmpub.com

ISBN 978-1-4938-2054-2

© 2016 Teacher Created Materials, Inc.
Printed in China
Nordica.082019.CA21901019

Words to Know

rain

snow

wind